√ 1-2013
Last CKO 3-29-12

OCT 0 6 2009

Guess Who
Hunts

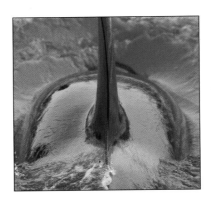

Dana Meachen Rau

 Marshall Cavendish
Benchmark
New York

I am big.

I live in the ocean.

My tail helps me swim fast.

It moves up and down.

My *flippers* help me steer.

I zoom through the water.

I hear well in the water.

I make clicking sounds.

My skin is smooth.

My skin is black and white.

I need air.

I swim to the surface of
the water.

My *blowhole* is on top of my head.

I breathe out. Whoosh!

My baby *calf* stays close.

I feed her with my milk.

I live in a group.

Our group is called a *pod*.

We hunt for food.

I spy a seal to eat.

We hunt for fish, too.

I grab one with my teeth.

You can see my fin above the water.

Who am I?

I am a whale!

Who am I?

blowhole

calf

fin

flippers

pod

skin   **tail**   **teeth**

Challenge Words

blowhole (BLOW-hole) The hole on a whale's head that helps it breathe.

calf (kaf) A baby whale.

flippers (FLIP-uhrs) The flat side fins of a whale.

pod A group of whales that live together.

Index

Page numbers in **boldface** are illustrations.

About the Author

Dana Meachen Rau is the author of many other titles in the Bookworms series, as well as other nonfiction and early reader books. She lives in Burlington, Connecticut, with her husband and two children.

With thanks to the Reading Consultants:

Nanci Vargus, Ed.D., is an Assistant Professor of Elementary Education at the University of Indianapolis.

Beth Walker Gambro is an Adjunct Professor at the University of St. Francis in Joliet, Illinois.

Marshall Cavendish Benchmark
99 White Plains Road
Tarrytown, New York 10591-5502
www.marshallcavendish.us

Library of Congress Cataloging-in-Publication Data

Rau, Dana Meachen, 1971–
Guess who hunts / by Dana Meachen Rau.
p. cm. — (Bookworms. Guess who)
Summary: "Following a guessing game format, this book provides young readers with
clues about a whale's physical characteristics, behaviors, and habitats, challenging readers
to identify it"—Provided by publisher.
Includes index.
ISBN 978-0-7614-2907-4
1. Whales—Juvenile literature. I. Title. II. Series.
QL737.C4R25 2009
599.5—dc22
2007024605

Editor: Christina Gardeski
Publisher: Michelle Bisson
Designer: Virginia Pope
Art Director: Anahid Hamparian

Photo Research by Anne Burns Images

Cover Photo by *Peter Arnold, Inc.*/R.Hicker

The photographs in this book are used with permission and through the courtesy of:
Corbis: pp. 1, 25, 28TR Tom Brakefield; pp. 5, 7, 28BL, 29C Brandon D. Cole;
pp. 13, 28TL Galen Rowell. *Minden Pictures*: pp. 3, 23, 29R Flip Nicklin.
Animals Animals: pp. 9, 17, 28TC Gerard Lacz; pp. 11, 29L Susan Beatty;
pp. 19, 28BR Suzi Eszterhas. *Peter Arnold*: p. 15 R. Hicker; p. 21 David McNew; p. 27 P. Wegner.

Printed in Malaysia
1 3 5 6 4 2